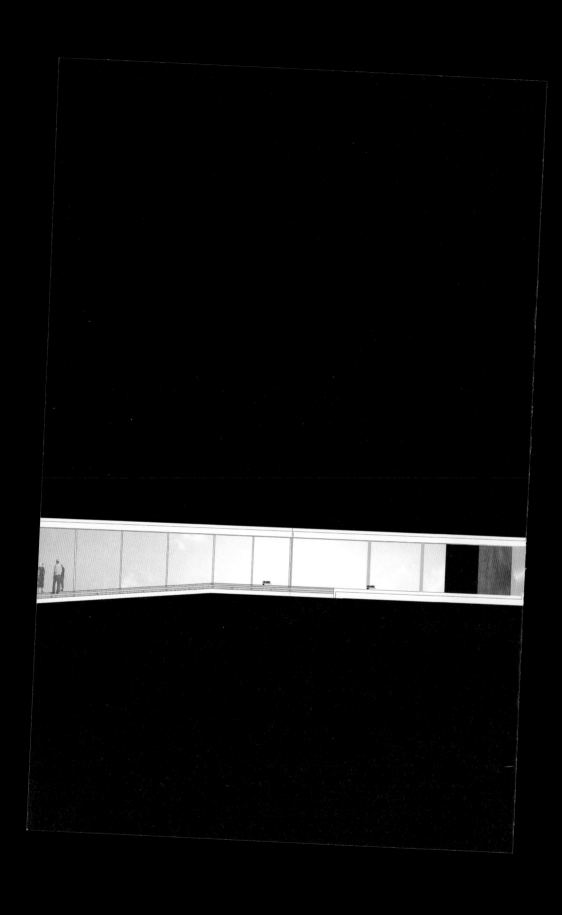

The Dutch Embassy in Berlin
by OMA / Rem Koolhaas

Contents

|

The Dutch Embassy in Berlin by OMA / Rem Koolhaas

NAi Publishers, Rotterdam

Plates [1]

Candida Höfer

C.H. (born in 1944) studied photography under Bernd and Hella Becher.
She has taken part in many group
exhibitions and has held countless solo
shows, most recently at the 50th Venice
Biennale at the German Pavilion.
Recently *Candida Höfer. A monograph*
was published.

8

18

Psychogeography of a Cube

The Dutch Embassy in Berlin

François Chaslin

F. C. (born in 1948) is an architect and architecture critic who teaches at the School of Architecture in Lille and produces a weekly radio show devoted to architecture on the French station Radio France-Culture. He is the author of numerous articles and publications amongst which *Deux conversations avec Rem Koolhaas, et cætera.*

The Dutch Embassy in Berlin is certainly a work in its own right: a virtuoso spatial *fantäsie* articulated within a limited, strictly cubic space, where it continually twists and turns upon itself. This playful and rather capricious exploration of the pleasures of complexity is an exacerbation of the theme of the architectural promenade; it constructs a controlled and joyful chaos. Several of the topological games which had already been developed by Rem Koolhaas and his followers are concentrated here, along a zigzag trajectory that folds back on itself several times within a perfectly modest-looking glass block measuring 27 metres square. There is something intriguing about this contrast between the internal vitality of the organism and the tranquil expression of its façades – like the reserve of a gentleman in the grip of a mounting excitement which he manages to keep carefully concealed (a diplomat, for example).

Koolhaas explains that he sought to realize a building which would allow us to 'understand Berlin better', thanks to an initiatory path that underscores several aspects, architectures and ambiances of the city. He wants to consider 'with equal seriousness' highly diverse elements of the German capital's historical context. Avoiding a spectacular expressionism, remaining on a kind of middle ground even while the building plays on a vibrant outburst, he has masked the real stakes behind a restful appearance, behind a guise of Dutch humanism and openness. Avoiding any repetitions, distancing himself from his followers, he surprises us once more with this exploration of a new precinct of infinite possibility. Because the possibilities are legion, and vertiginous as soon as one opens the door; but the constant clamour of these infinite spaces fascinates us today, and no longer provokes any dread.

To begin with, then, the embassy is a somewhat distanced response to a political situation and a historical context. But also to two national images, two quests for identity, at least one of which is rather tormented. On one side you have the idea of openness, of modernity, of transparency, which is supposed to characterize the Netherlands; on the other, a reunified Germany dealing as well as possible with its lugubrious past, its haunting trauma, palpable everywhere in the urban framework, in its ruins, its voids, its incompletion, in its physical scars, and in the coexistence of architectural types, styles and atmospheres which are all unbelievably foreign to each other. To be sure, there is a particular beauty to this environment shaped by historical tragedy, yet it is at the same time so alive, so much freer to invent the future than certain other cities which did not suffer and which now tend to suffocate beneath their ancient trappings. Yet in Germany's eyes this environment can only signify its own absence as a nation, as an entity, its humiliating dispersion into discordant fragments.

Berlin wishes to rediscover that period when, as heir to one of Europe's finest civilizations, it embodied the great city, the *Großstadt*, opulent and not yet guilty. It wants to offer a homogeneous cityscape, without any gaps, stitched perfectly together again without any residual stretches of no man's land. This cityscape from which the traces of Nazism have almost totally disappeared now seeks to blur those of both Communism and the Western modernism of the fifties and sixties, held in equal antipathy. As though these were two faces of the same drama. As though the long period of the Cold War, the partition of the country for forty years, from 1949 to 1989 (and the existence of the Wall for over twenty-eight years, from August 13, 1961, to November 9, 1989), had only resulted in a double disintegration of Berlin's soul, putting the final touches on the annihilation of German memory by the Second World War.

The Netherlands wanted an autonomous, singular, clearly legible embassy, and if possible, an event. The Berlin authorities thought that the building should efface itself behind the common rule, for they aim to erect this cityscape through the imposition of a somewhat artificial regulatory model, which they call Critical Reconstruction.

The traditional urban fabric of this agglomeration had been destroyed by the bombardments, the battles of 1945, the final collapse of the Reich and all that followed, but also by the systematic installation of a motorway network and the great slash of the Wall. Today the authorities lay equal responsibility on the modernist and functionalist ideology ingrained by Hans Scharoun in particular, who was *Stadtbaurat*, or municipal architect, after 1945. His distant successor, the current *Senatsbaudirektor* Hans Stimmann, director of the Construction and Housing department of the Berlin Senate, evaluates the history of the city as 'a history of destruction, by the war and by the planners after the war'. And recently one could read a

28

sentence by the writer Ernst Jünger (from *Autor und Autorschaft*, 1984) placed as an epigraph to a cartographic work: 'Our city centres have been more severely damaged by architects than by bombs. The worst a bomb can do is to damage a building's substance and raze it to the ground, but the architect destroys its essence from the ground upwards.' A condemnation recalling the remarks of Prince Charles in December 1987, in his Mansion House speech at the height of his campaign against modern architecture, when he declared that one could at least give some credit to the *Luftwaffe*, as compared to the English architects: 'when it knocked down our buildings, it didn't replace them with anything more offensive than rubble.'

Two clans of city planners face off in Berlin. They launch mutual accusations of negationism, and reproach each other for seeking to conceal aspects of the city's heritage. One group speaks of an eternal genius of Berlin, a kind of essence inscribed in the tracery of its streets, in its typomorphology. Their opponents accuse them of trying to cover up Nazism, the city's destruction, the communist experiment and the two post-war periods, both of them modernist, unfolding in parallel after the brief parenthesis of socialist realism with the Stalinallee: the shared memory of half a century. Each group refers to irreconcilable pasts, one looking further back into history, the other to a more burning actuality. For Hans Stimmann, 'post-war architects, planners and politicians lived with a hatred of the past and a belief in progress, in both East and West'.

Here, in this antagonism, this crisis of viewpoints, is where Rem Koolhaas can infiltrate. He often quotes the watchword of the Haus-Rücker group from Austria: 'amnesty for the existent'. It is a call for us to admit that other periods and cultures, and even very recent ones, have produced fragments of cities and buildings which we can tolerate today, without any compulsive denigration.

Among the concerns of those responsible for Berlin's city planning, there is the fractured aspect of the lot structure. Stimmann and his colleagues no longer find the slightest 'fabric' that could assure the cohesion of the centre. No longer do we see any of that fine-grained texture whose density and regularity the connoisseurs of the city so appreciate in the aerial photographs of yesteryear, or in the 'black plans' whose concept Josef Paul Kleihues had discovered, during the heyday of postmodernism and the *Internationale Bauanstel-*

lung, in the famous work Collage City by Colin Rowe and Fred Koetter, published shortly before then in 1978.

City planners, in Rowe and Koetter's view, are caught between their nostalgia for the traditional city and the reality of the modern metropolis, which has become a 'mass of visually disparate objects', because the street has disintegrated. They compare a plan of the Italian city of Parma – densely black, tightly interwoven, broken only by infrequent plazas and alleyways – with Le Corbusier's plan for the reconstruction of Saint-Dié. At the source of this technique for the reading of urban reality lies the plan of Rome published in 1748 by Giambattista Nolli. This icon of postmodernism already depicted the buildings in black, leaving the streets, plazas, porches and courtyards reserved in white, as well as the outline of the palaces, churches and public buildings. Colin Rowe knew very well that the architectural object would not wither away and dissolve so easily, but he called for its assimilation into a 'texture'.

Mounted in the year 2000 under the tutelage of Hans Stimmann and Tobias Nöfer as part of the Venice Biennial, the exhibition Physiognomie einer Großstadt displayed an eloquent collection of these black plans. The Senatsbaudirektor considered them to represent 'a critical analysis of the spatial ideas of architectural modernism after 1945'. The series meticulously described the texture of Berlin at five key moments: at the outset of the war, in 1940; shortly after the disaster, in 1953; at the fall of the Wall, in 1989; in the year 2000; and one decade after that. For each of these periods, black, blue and red lines bring out the existing structures along with those which have been destroyed, newly built, or projected for the future. A second series of plans used line drawings to sketch the transformation of the lot structure.

Another obsessively recurrent question in Berlin today is the Who's Who, the catalogue or encyclopaedia of the international architects who by dozens since the war have left the traces of their passage, so many samples of the fashions or stylistic preoccupations of a given moment – and not only for grand occasions such as the Hansa-Viertel quarter of Interbau 57, the buildings of the Internationale Bauausstellung, Iba 87, or the constructive surges of the 1990s. All the rationalisms, the more or less participatory expressionisms, the postmodernisms, deconstructivisms or minimalisms have their

30

representatives in Berlin. All the techniques are there: the hyperbolic paraboloids, the architectonic or brutalist concrete, the metal skeletons, the facades in coloured plastic or stone, with curtain walls or asbestos cement, gilt aluminium or glued glass. The result is a treasure trove of examples, a kind of architectural collection, but it also nourishes something like a complex of the colonized. Therefore Hans Stimmann has decided that the city should no longer pursue 'the goal of re-inventing Berlin' but should draw instead on the resources of 'built history' as it unfolded before the arrival of this bric-a-brac eclecticism: the history of a solid city of stone, that *steinerne Berlin* described – but mockingly at the time – by Werner Hegemann in a volume published in 1930. For a European city centre supposedly needs materiality, 'walls and openings that mark the transition between building and city, private and public'.

No longer an exemplar of the International Style, this European city should refer to a reactivated local tradition: it calls 'for office and commercial buildings to take up premodernist and modernist architectural traditions'. It should 'lend Berlin's particular colours to the international architectural idiom', by taking back 'the historical street pattern and the historical building lines of the roads and squares'. No matter if this is to be felt as 'an affront to those architects who are used to working without being restricted by rules and regulations'.

Yet a ticklish problem remains, concerning the destiny of what had been East Berlin. Unexpectedly, a peculiar nostalgia has rapidly developed for the communist period: it is called *ostalgia*. Public opinion has become much more complex. And the strength of the project for the Dutch Embassy is to have taken up this many-sided quarrel in a deftly understated way, behind the simple appearance of a glass cube, a discreet façade where most will see only banality.

When Berlin prepared to become the capital of Germany again in January 2000, a small number of countries chose not to install their representatives around the Tiergarten or the Pariserplatz, but rather in the old centre on its way to reconstitution, along the banks of the Spree, upriver from the Fischerinsel. This Fishermen's Island had long been the geographic heart of the modest seventeenth-century agglomeration, when it was fortified and surrounded by moats, before it developed the neoclassical extensions of Dorotheen-

stadt and Friedrichstadt, and then became the capital of the kingdom of Prussia in 1701. Thus on the left side where the Jannowitz
bridge strikes land there is the Chinese embassy, gleaming and stolid
and paradoxically Germanic, wrapped in stainless steel like a bank;
and then a few steps further along the quay is the elegant Brazilian
embassy, whose slim horizontal balconies are more suggestive of a
wealthy private residence.

The upper quay is bordered with old, rather closed-in admin-
istrative buildings, which may well be from the Nazi period. They
have steep roofs, and dark spots marked by impacts; not so many
years ago they still housed the Ministry of Culture of the German
Democratic Republic, the seat of the *Jugendarbeit* organisation and the
services of the Mint. A little further along, at the corner of the quay
and the Klosterstraße, the senatorial Finance Administration occu-
pies a building with a frankly National-Socialist aesthetic, with its
jutting cornice, travertine base, pale grey roughcast finish and stone
frames for the windows and the porch with its five arcades.

There used to be vacant lots and warehouses here, workshops
and garages. The cluster was filled in with the building of a headquarters for the Berlin water company. At the curve of Stralauer
Straße, in the now-dissolved space of what once had been the
picturesque Molken Markt square, it displays a kind of Gothic porch
done in an old Czech cubist or expressionist style, with four levels
stuck like a kind of dark concrete rood screen before a six-storey
edifice in the form of a barrel, covered with zinc cladding. The
remainder of the company inhabits a hulking building on which
strips of dull stone alternate with polished marble on a strictly
ordered façade. False chimney bases lend rhythm to the two levels of
attics, while three strong undulations of the structure and a number
of glass accents are supposed to evoke the theme of the water along
the Neue Jüdenstraße. This complex is at once austere, opulent, and
marked by the standards of Critical Reconstruction. It is organized as
called for in the rules around small square courtyards of a little less
than 20 metres on a side, with a façade that gives way at 22 metres
to the cornice, and does not exceed 27 metres at the roof crest.

It is a strange moment being played out here: the reconstruction
of a city that never really existed in this form, the pursuit of the history of an ideal capital which is supposed never to have undergone

the traumas of the War and the Wall. Or which seeks to forget them.

Yet facing the quay, behind the weeping willows and the trees-of-heaven, the ancient Fishermen's Island, formerly crisscrossed with streets full of tightly huddled little buildings, now boasts six collective housing blocks, six towers some 25 stories high, which at the close of the 1960s transformed the island into a kind of edge city. The maps and the aerial photographs prior to the destruction bear witness to the atmosphere of what has since become a green space. Faced with the impossibility of destroying these towers with their hundreds of apartments, and still attempting to conform to the doctrine contained in the plans of the 1990s (the *Gesamtberliner Flächennutzungplan*, the master plan of the entire agglomeration, applied since 1994, and *Planwerk Innenstadt*, established for the city centre in 1996), the current directives propose at least to reconstitute the streets, with seven or eight clusters of buildings around courtyards, and also to construct sequences of buildings aligned on the avenue of the Gertraudenstraße and the quay of the Friedrichsgracht. The Ahornblatt restaurant complex has already been razed; the expressive forms of this huge building, whose five hyperbolic paraboloids earned it the name of Maple Leaf, must have seemed to hail from a dated and disagreeably communist modernism.

Dieter Hoffmann-Axthelm explains how the *Planwerk Innenstadt*, a mosaic of projects which bear equally on both the former East and West sectors of the city, is in reality addressed to two very different worlds, both in terms of their physiognomy and of their future roles. The first, fashioned by 'bourgeois culture', is essentially destined to 'enhance the value of the individual urban spaces with additional architecture'. The second, which constituted the political centre of the German Democratic Republic, is characterised by low density, overly wide streets and disproportionately large public spaces, 'which have no use today'. It is slated to serve as a historical centre for the city as a whole, making it necessary to lay 'a new text over the socialist modernism of the GDR centre'.

But as Hoffmann-Axthelm admits, the plan gave rise to great controversy, with many intellectuals in the East seeing it as nothing less than a form of colonization. And certain Western city planners experienced it as an attack on various positive aspects of modernism to which they remained attached (particularly the automobile).

Nonetheless, he assures that the project does not involve any indiscriminate destruction. That on the contrary, its principle is the respect of the existent. That it does not intend to demolish the city left by Communism, if only because the modern space resists, because it 'excludes change by its very exclusivity'. That the open character of the environment will remain legible, but simply will be filled in, tightened up, infiltrated by another urban material, by a second built layer which, to a certain degree, will bring it closer to the proportions and scale of the historical city.

For this sector of Berlin-Mitte, the projects of the administration directed by Hans Stimmann are not limited to reconstructing one end of Fishermen's Island. They also foresee rebuilding the Waisen-Brücke, which doubled the Jannowitz bridge all the way to the post-war period, and flanking the MülenBrücke with a construction recalling the old industrial mill of former times. The Breite Straße, whose gentle curve cannot be restored, will become narrower, to the detriment of the façade of the Bauwesen building (the Construction Ministry of the former GDR). As for the ancient castle of the Hohenzollern, razed in 1950, the Bundestag voted for the reconstruction of three of its facades in July 2002, the fourth being more or less embedded in the communist Palace of the Republic, the *Palast der Republik*, which some call *Ballast der Republik*, as it is laced with asbestos and slated for destruction in a will to eradicate the fundamental symbols of the old regime.

The official project is therefore one of 'reurbanizing', of filling in the entire centre and attempting to restore some of its former lot structure (even though it was highly fragmented in the past), if not to restore its architecture as seen in the engravings, the old photographs, or the papier-mâché model that a fervent partisan of the castle's reconstruction has made available for the passers-by in a display window on Unter den Linden, showing the disparate and picturesque, almost medieval character of the ornate facades, the gables, the skylights, the balustrades and the diversely sloping roofs.

The same process also applies to the right bank of the Spree, in the district of the city hall, the Rotes Rathaus, and all the way to Alexanderplatz which, on the contrary, will see the rise of a powerful group of historicizing skyscrapers, designed in 1993 by Hans Kollhoff. As for the future site of the Dutch Embassy, it was supposed

34

to be reconstructed like a traditional Berlin block. According to the *Planwerk Innenstadt* in its May 1999 version, as adopted by the Senate and the municipal Parliament, this cluster behind the corner of a square installed on the quay was to be treated with an enclosed organization of buildings around five quite small square courtyards, augmented by a larger one.

The first trick that OMA has played on this rule – carried out thanks to a certain benevolence of the local city planning officials, heirs to the tradition of the East – is an unprecedented combination of block and independent building. The embassy is not exactly set down on the ground, but partially on a pedestal, a kind of *piano nobile* or terrace. It does not share a wall with the neighbouring facades, but remains isolated. It is not made of stone but of glass. A first, L-shaped building, slightly out of line and expanded to form a slightly obtuse angle, is there to ensure the transition. It is propped against the water company headquarters and contains five apartments. Exactly 27 metres high as per the rulebook, with a narrow façade of only some 3 metres (and only half of that along the Klosterstraße), it is entirely sheathed in a grillwork of perforated aluminium plates which renders it slightly abstract. Its transparency plays with the light and, depending on the hour of the day, it allows one to glimpse the shadow of the floors, terraces and staircases, the cross-arms of the bracing, the underpinnings of the façades, the air-conditioning tubes and ducts, and sometimes a fragment of the neighbouring building, lit up by a ray of sun that goes on to lose itself among the linden trees of a small courtyard.

So this is what remains of the cluster: a pedestal and a rather diaphanous backdrop, at once volume and curtain. In plan, the glass cube is slightly skewed, as though escaping from the open hand formed by the angle – as though the Berlin block were relaxing its grip. A void surrounds it, a dynamic void, a moving and slightly spiral void which serves as an automobile access ramp from the Klosterstraße. This empty space frees the building, disengaging it as though it had been cut out from the mass of the cluster. Then the void penetrates it brusquely at the first floor, on the level of the foyer, and rolls up within it in the form of the interior 'trajectory', in a jerky, irregular ascent. From the embassy reception hall to the roof, it measures over 200 metres.

Almost three years before the Berlin project was developed, OMA had already imagined this kind of device, in a more organic, pliable and curving topology. It was in 1993, on the occasion of the competition for the twin libraries at the University of Jussieu, in Paris. Certain zones of each floor plan rose up to connect the levels with a continuous itinerary, traversing the totality of the structure like 'a warped interior boulevard' so that the visitor could remain in contact with the different spaces of the libraries and the surrounding landscape. A moving ground unfolded, a 'flying carpet' between the stacked and inextricably mingled floors, opening its path through the skeleton of the building. Here it deployed a ramp, there a more sinuous slope, a hollow, a rounded butte, or there again a roof, a vault evoking a fragment of a dome.

In this case the trajectory is linear and more angular, with fractures, a series of cavities that seem to be cut with a pickaxe from the volume of the cube, a chain of shadows and lights, of reflections and colours. Rem Koolhaas has undertaken a quiet polemic here against the current taste for bubbles, for the formless or the spongy. In the circumvolutions of these meandering worlds elaborated with computers, one ceaselessly explores space, permanent and mobile. Here the space is also self-identical and always different, but within a firmer and more material extension, which is also more practicable, and stackable as well. The superimposition creates chance events along the way, as though knotted within the hollow of the block. The floor is also the ceiling, each ramp or stairway becomes an occasion for concentrations or dilations of the corridor itself, and of the rooms between which it glides on its path through the mass of the cube, from storey to storey. Inside it is lined with mat aluminium, on the floor, walls and ceilings. A metallic ambience guides you to the nooks and crannies of the itinerary and introduces a continuous relation to the light. On the outside, seen from whatever room it brushes against, it is sheathed in dark wood, Brazilian copaiva with wide veins, slightly split and reddish, installed vertically but for the exception of the main room. Elsewhere, another tropical species, bordering on yellow – zebrano wood with its finer and more contrasting veins – is used in horizontal beds.

An orderly visit to the embassy would begin with the most public place, the consulate, installed on the ground floor like a

36

showcase, in an open gallery set back from the Klosterstraße and running parallel to it. Here the counters are made of an immense plate of translucent resin, extremely luminous, in a lime green or 'linden' colour; you find the same material at the reception desk, in pale pink, and at the internal post office on the seventh floor, once again in linden. On the floor is aluminium gridding, on the ceiling too: the trajectory has begun. A sculpted bronze plate bears the kingdom's coat of arms, two upright lions holding a shield with the motto of the princes of Orange, *Je maintiendrai*. It was transferred from the earlier locations of the embassy, in Bonn, then on the twenty-first floor of a kind of skyscraper in the Friedrichstraße.

At either side, two narrow staircases lead to the first floor, which is the real reception level, on the balcony-courtyard that supports the building and looks out at the Spree beyond the acacia trees. Leading up to it is a broad inclined plane, a ramp of asphalt offered to the urban space. A formidable window begins at the right, 8 to 10 metres high: it is diagonal, bevelled in a powerful gesture which opens up towards the direction of the Stralauer Straße behind us. Above – but one can hardly see it – another hole has been pierced through the northern wing, a deformed square more than 5 metres square. It plays an essential role in the device and constitutes a kind of oblique sight which, from the square of the Rolandufer quay, guides your eye through the trajectory hollowed into the cube and then onward to the gilt sphere or Sputnik of the 365 metre-high television tower some 700 metres away – the *Fernsehturm* constructed in the late 1960s on the edge of Alexanderplatz, the very emblem of communist Berlin. Higher up, four gangways of reinforced concrete bridge the gap, linking the cube to the apartments superimposed in the corner of the L-shaped building; they are partially veiled by the grillwork of perforated aluminium, and partially open, with broad expanses of windows, drapes and blinds.

Tubes of galvanized metal, pipeline style, stand out like body-guards along the back opening and terrace. Here we are at the base of the building, the *piano nobile*, facing the entryway. The façade is composed of two broad glass walls, which include occasional sliding elements, and also of plates of black-lacquered steel bearing a large number 50, the address of the building below on the Klosterstraße, with a white horizontal line that adds *AmbassadevanhetKoninkrijkder,*

'Royal Embassy', and then continues with *Nederlanden*, 'of the Netherlands', inscribed on a panel that slides open to serve as a door.

The furniture in the upper room of the reception hall, with its
ceiling of sloping aluminium, is by Marcel Wanders. On the right, a
very narrow passageway, shrunken to 1.2 metres, betrays the presence of an enormous protuberance, an upthrust of concrete that
rises almost 9 metres inside the building. Three steps, and you
descend into the multipurpose room, which opens up full south
though a 14-metre show window. A long Jacquard curtain, double-
sided and reversible, can be drawn along the window; it bears a
botanical motif, an angelica branch in forthright hues, sharp green
and white on the river side; white, dark blue and grey on the drapes
of another bay window in the back.

Oblique views come from the Internet space, lodged in a
mezzanine. Others can be glimpsed through mirrors covered with
red film: a moment of the trajectory as it zigzags between two higher
floors. An isolated rectangular post leans like a titan; it is massive and
springs from the ground floor in a dark cloakroom of the consulate,
traversing the lower levels and dissolving around the fourth or fifth.
The structure of the building is empirical, random, practically
impossible to describe, difficult to imagine or sketch; and the
models, opaque and overcharged, can only convey a vague idea. It
is a baroque organism of reinforced concrete, irregular, constituted
of sudden concentrations of mass, shrinkages, slabs, girders, poured
walls which are sometimes quite thick, cantilevers and boxes (a
black box in the decoding room, the boxes of staircases and elevators), inclined pilings and girders that are straight, round, wide or
thin, with breaks and ruptures of all kinds.

In the left-hand corner of the entryway at the edge of the
reception hall is the reinforced glass box of the security guards,
marking the departure point of the inside trajectory, the private
zone of the embassy. Views extend down below, at high or low
angles, into the corners beneath the staircase. The elevators are vertical, in the usual manner, and their translucent walls glide past vertical tubes of neon fixed inside the dark shaft. One tube and it's the
first level, then two, three, all the way to eleven tubes in gradually
mounting bedazzlement. The 200-metre itinerary begins here.
Sometimes sloping, sometimes flat, it slips through floors whose

38

ceiling heights vary from 2.15 or 2.3 to around 6 metres.

The trajectory cleaves its pathway. A long landing with brushed aluminium flooring, an initial frontal view towards the travertine-framed windows of the old Nazi building, and then it moves through a glass box jutting out like an oriel window beyond the façade, up a sharp green mirror-ramp that plays games with the morning light. Next comes a wide landing, a broad angled girder that tilts for obscure structural reasons. The way the different levels fold and cross changes the physiognomy of the trajectory. It is distorted by its own movements. They leave their mark on the aluminium-clad floors and ceilings, they destabilize the lateral walls. At times the glass-paned interior partitions are lined in coloured film. Behind an orange mirror, a passageway to the archives on the second floor, long and folded. Behind a translucent red partition, a glance below extends towards the multipurpose room; at the bottom, the Internet space, the quays, the acacia branches. Here is a piece of the glass roof, pale salmon pink. It looks somehow like a kind of coffer in an office. Elsewhere, a yellow passageway. The trajectory follows the south façade for a few metres, then strikes into the very heart of the cube for a new ascent. Steps and counter-steps in aluminium, irregular landings, narrowings, accordion-like partitions. In the distance a cut of light: we are in the sightline, with the sphere of the huge Sputnik in our own line of vision.

Everything interlocks, tightens up, freezes into the secret of a Chinese puzzle, a woodworker's masterpiece, dovetailed assemblages, mortises and tenons. On the left, a meeting room in fainter light, no windows, rather sombre, high triangular forms. A round oculus cut into the floor looks down at the ceiling of the reception hall through a kind of well. A nook in the back, just a few steps and you find a shortcut between offices. A room at the right behind a door, thick like a safe. On the facing wall, 'peep-show' wallpaper by Droog Design: a grid of dots in different diameters, like kinetic art. The dots are not painted but punched into the paper, and the holes show the raw concrete with its creamy material that crops up again on numerous walls, ceilings and beams, and on certain large sliding doors, all plastered over in the same tones.

The trajectory suddenly broadens when between the sixth and seventh floors it opens out at the northern wall into a landing dazzled in the light reflected by the façade of aluminium grillwork. Post office and archiving rooms. In front of us is one of the access gangways to the annex. Into the cut-out of the sightline floats the slow movement of a poplar tree, the television tower expands, the cityscape enlarges to encompass the lantern and the slate dome of the Stadthaus, an extension of the city hall built at the outset of the last century by the official architect Ludwig Hoffmann.

The trajectory snakes around a dark recess, renewing its ascent within the cube, towards the south this time, in the form of a new fresh slope. It is crossed by a glassed-in gangway. A view below. Five steps to the right marks the entry to the ambassador's office: travertine flooring with a mysterious black box in our line of vision, cantilevered at the eighth level above the void. It is a meeting room where ten people can gather around a table. From this overhanging room one sees the quays, the houseboats, and farther away among the trees, the towers of Fisherman's Island. Outside, the human presences and V-shaped structure of the skeleton are glimpsed through smoky limousine windows.

For the second time, the trajectory has come up against the smooth southern facade, transparent with its glass stiffeners. A broad staircase rises in two flights. At the landing midway between, a large door, or more precisely, a pivoting partition, opens up to the news and relaxation room, and also to a series of offices. At the back of this floor is a small amphitheatre of three steps in a corner, resting on the frame of the sightline.

The trajectory crooks an elbow. Broader steps, slighter slope, the itinerary ends with a ramp that runs along the façade and the roofs of the senatorial Finance Administration one last time, then makes its final ascent. It passes alongside the fitness club, situated in fainter light, stepped back from the facades but with a variety of different views, masked by mirrors and pieces of one-way glass. Enter the club and the south façade, a long strip of amphitheatre like a final ramp that runs into the ceiling slab; it will make an auditorium or a place to wait on the steps.

40   On the last landing, the stairway slips into a more restricted perspective – it's the entry to the canteen. The ceiling is more industrial in character, with a frame and steel basins. Partly uncovered, it slides back to reveal a gap towards the sky, allowing access to the

terrace by an openwork staircase. To the south, from the apartment of the ambassador's deputy, or from the terraces of the personnel, you enjoy the full spectacle of the city, the tile roofs, the landscape of the collective housing complexes in the distance, the chimneys of a power station, the Brazilian and Chinese embassies, and right nearby, the mass of dark bricks, the high attic of patinated bronze and the pinnacles of the Märkisches Museum, the historical museum of Brandenburg, built in the early years of the last century by the same Ludwig Hoffmann. The panorama reveals a city extraordinarily more chaotic and dispersed than the one imagined by the exponents of Critical Reconstruction.

All this agitation, this spatial experimentation, unfolds in great inner tumult but without much reaction from the cube. Its façade is formed of a succession of glass coffers, arranged in a raster about 1.5 metres wide, with approximately half a metre's depth from one glass plate to the other; one of each two vertical posts is weight-bearing, while the other holds a small shutter (indeed, there is an entire system of ventilation between the coffers and the tunnel of the trajectory, whose slightly higher pressure allows it to serve as an air duct for the interior spaces). The differing heights of the floors introduce a kind of horizontal lamination, but barely perceptible from the outside, upon which the transformations of the façade are superimposed. At each incursion of the inner trajectory to the building's edge, the vertical structure fades and the façade becomes a huge single-block showcase, with a different glass, non-reflecting, using inside stiffeners of metal or flat glass plates. Overhanging the rest of the cube, a darker, smoother and more transparent box appears, underscored by aluminium edging. The latter forms a frame for the great bay window of the multipurpose room below, revealing effects of ramps or staircases, nuances of movements, subtle instabilities.

A filter, a thin veil of stretched metal, has been glued onto the bay windows of the south side. It captures the sunlight, mutes the contrasts and gilds the façade with a creamy tone. A darker, non-reflective glass underscores the set-back consulate, the box of the main room, the occasional protrusions of the trajectory, and the apartments of the upper storey, which seem to form a crest.

Difficult to grasp on the plans, or even when unfolded as a

cut-out model in cardboard, flattened like a pigeon for the grill, the trajectory is a curious space modelled in three dimensions. There is something active and nervous about it. We are far from the contemplative and slightly narcissistic vision that Le Corbusier formulated in 1925 concerning the device that he had just put into effect for the villa of the collector La Roche, in Auteuil. Of the house as a whole, he wrote that it would be 'like a *promenade architecturale*'; this was the first appearance of the expression. 'You enter: the architectural spectacle appears immediately to the gaze; you follow an itinerary and the perspectives unfold with great variety; you play with the flux of light illuminating the walls or casting zones of penumbra.'

Some five or six years later, while finishing the Savoye villa in Poissy, he mixed functional arguments and, strangely enough, the turning radius of a vehicle, with a kind of pedagogy of perfectly mastered space. 'You go right to the door of the house in an automobile', he noted in the second volume of his *Complete Works*, 'and it is the arc of the car's tightest turn that furnishes the very dimension of the house. The automobile advances beneath the pilings, turns around the shared services, arrives in the middle at the door of the vestibule, enters the garage and continues its path to return: there is the basic given.... The house will be set down in the grass like an object, without troubling anything.... It's when you walk, when you move that you see the architectural orders unfold.... In this house, it is a matter of a veritable architectural promenade, offering constantly varied aspects, unexpected and sometimes astonishing. It is interesting to offer so much diversity when, for example, from the constructive viewpoint one has admitted an absolutely rigorous schema of posts and beams.'

We are three-quarters of a century away from this Cartesian constructive rigor, spatial and sensorial. For as it was freed from horizontality, from references to the ancestral gait of humanity, from the rule of well-balanced staircases, as it was bent to ever more open and even somewhat perverse situations, plunged into disequilibrium and curved into Moebius strips, badgered into broken and embroiled topologies, in the end the architectural promenade had to be fully emancipated. It had to strike out for a life of its own, complete autonomy. It had to risk, no longer serving the space and its functions, but submitting them to itself. It had to verge on accidents.

42

And then it would be up to the rest of the architecture to adjust, to slip into the gaps, structures and spaces, to let itself be 'distributed' as well as possible by this impetuous zigzag.

Trajectory

Unfolded plan of the trajectory
with the trajectory areas in gray.
The circles indicate turning points
in the trajectory.

Scale 1/275

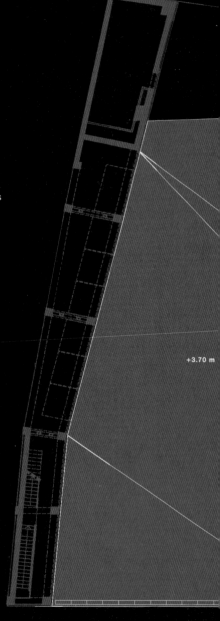

+3.70 m

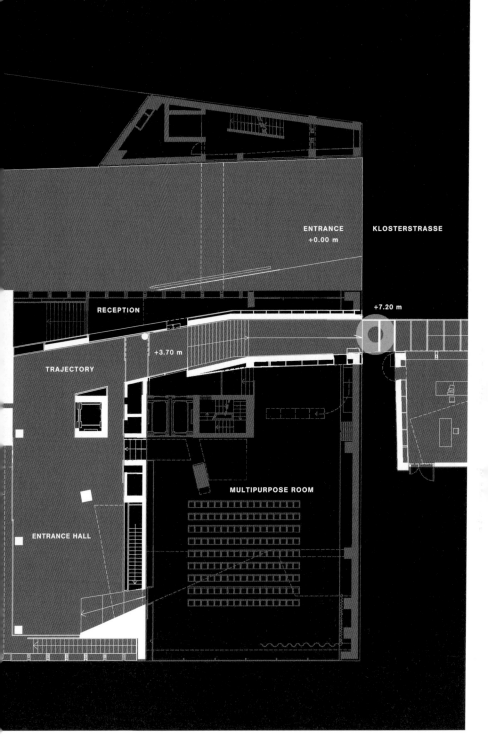

ENTRANCE
+0.00 m

KLOSTERSTRASSE

RECEPTION

+7.20 m

+3.70 m

TRAJECTORY

MULTIPURPOSE ROOM

ENTRANCE HALL

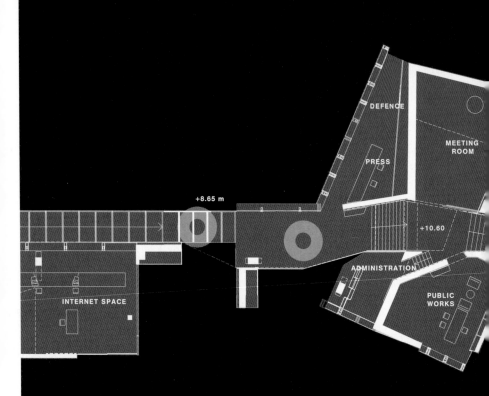

INTERNET SPACE

+8.65 m

DEFENCE

PRESS

MEETING ROOM

+10.60

ADMINISTRATION

PUBLIC WORKS

46

Trajectory

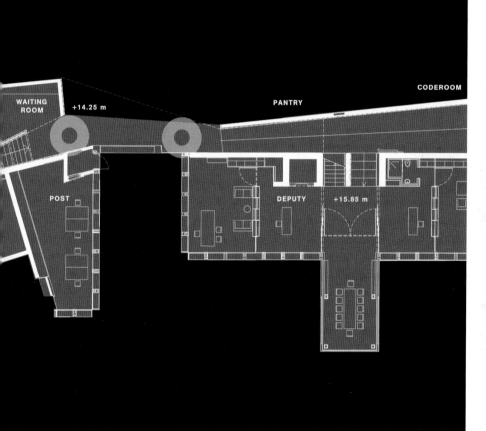

WAITING
ROOM
+14.25 m

PANTRY

CODEROOM

POST

DEPUTY   +15.85 m

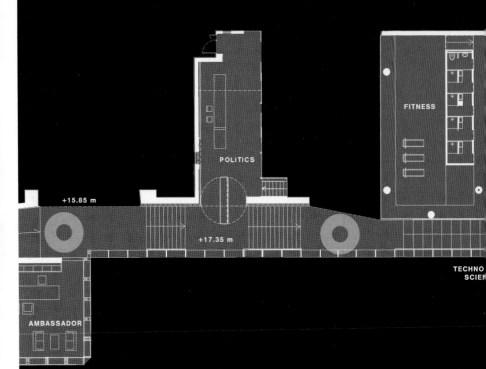

FITNESS

POLITICS

+15.85 m

+17.35 m

TECHNO
SCIEN

AMBASSADOR

48

Trajectory

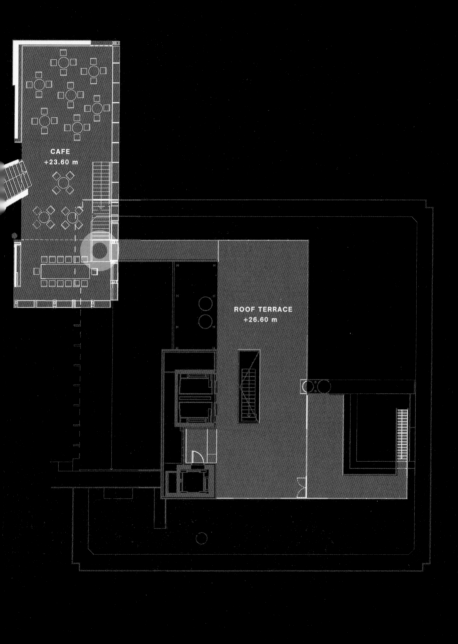

CAFE
+23.60 m

ROOF TERRACE
+26.60 m

Levels and Sections

Plans of the levels and sections with
the level and section areas in gray.

Scale 1/400

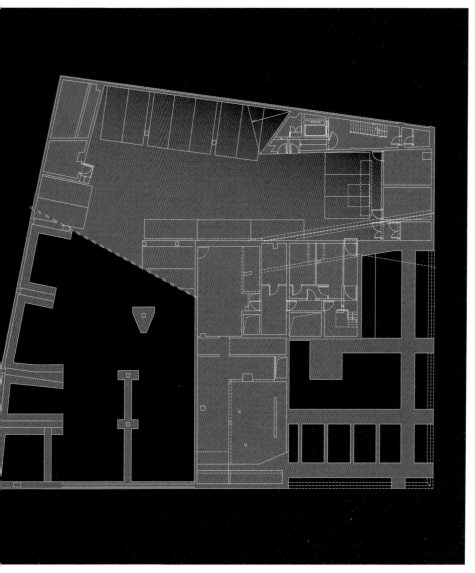

Level -1 Basement (-2.80 m)

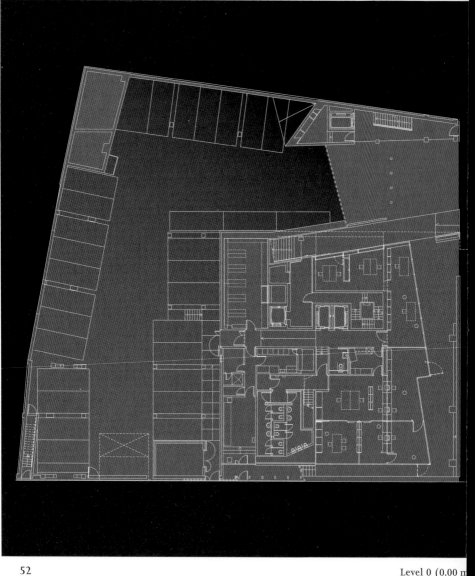

Level 0 (0.00 m

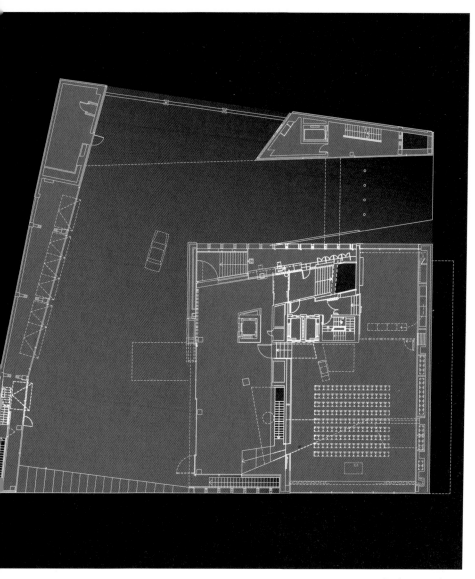

Level 1 (+3.70 m)

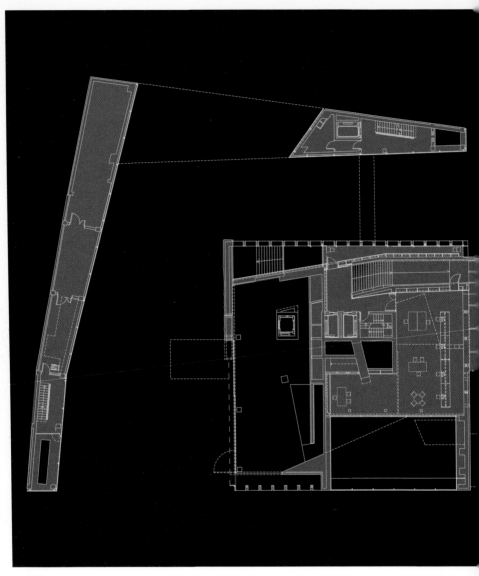

Level 2 (+7.20 m

Levels and Sections

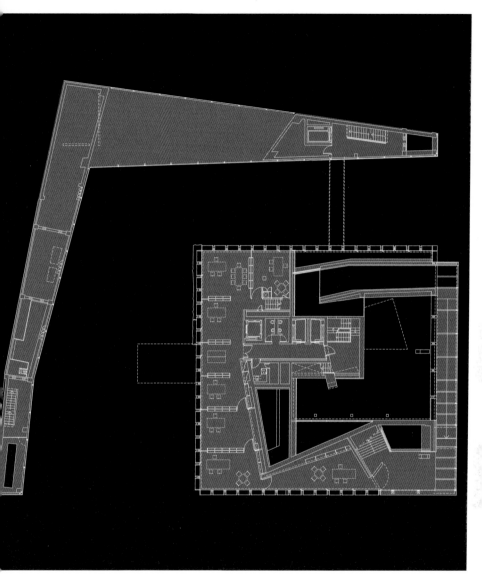

Level 3 (+8.65 m)

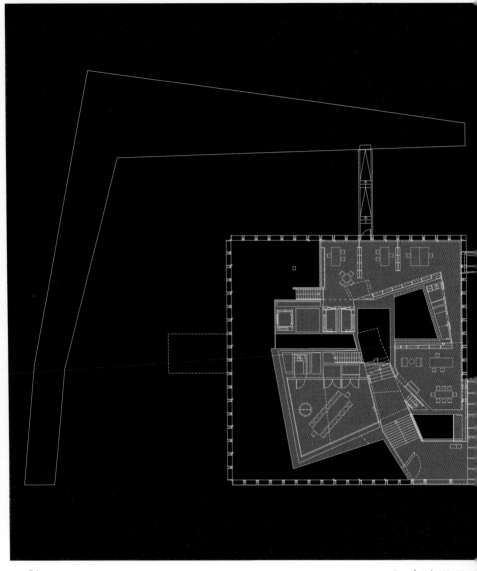

Level 4 (+10.60 m

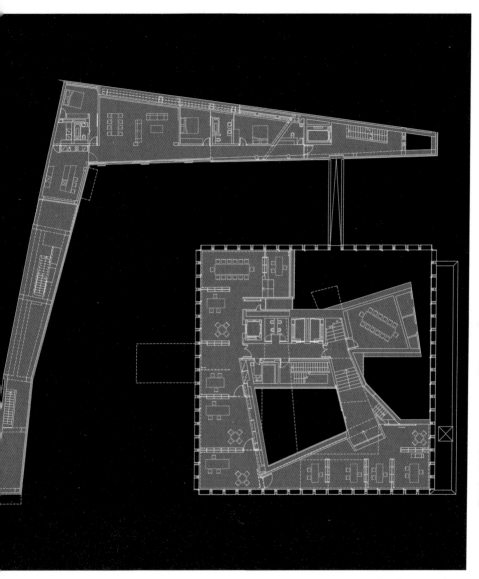

Level 5 (+11.75 m)

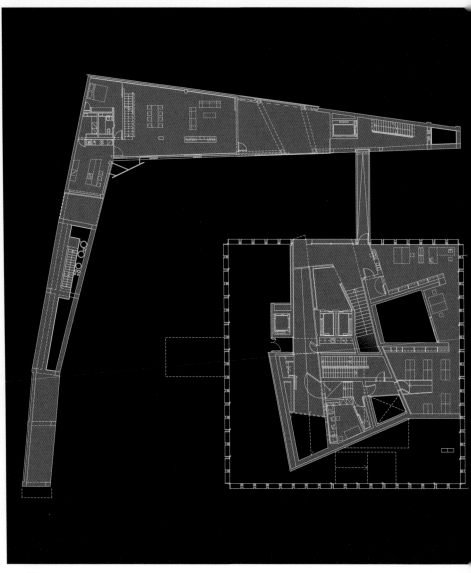

Level 6 (+14.25 r

Level 7 (+15.85 m)

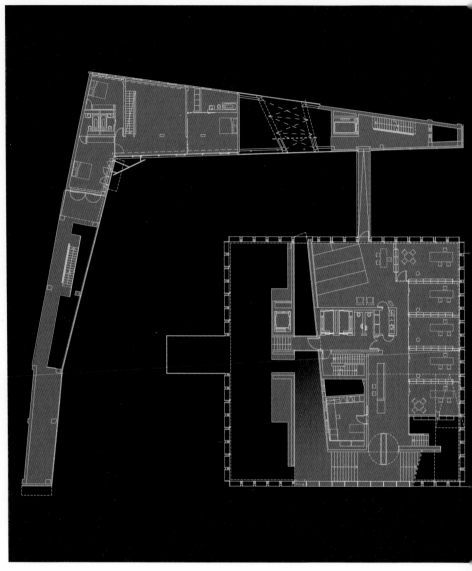

Level 8 (+17.35 r

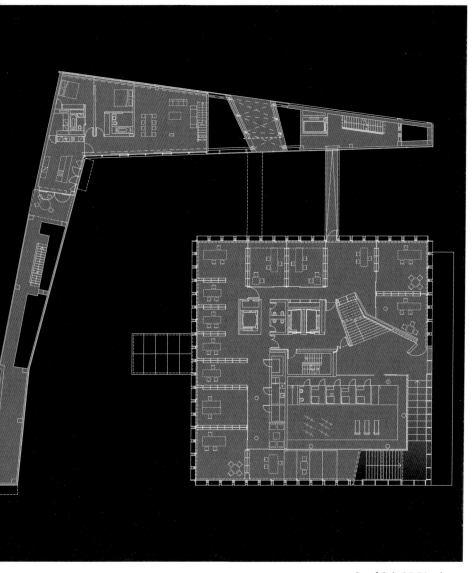

Level 9 (+20.50 m)

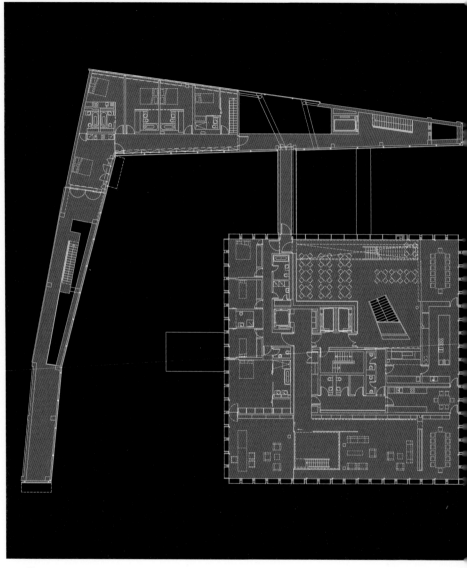

Level 10 (+23.60

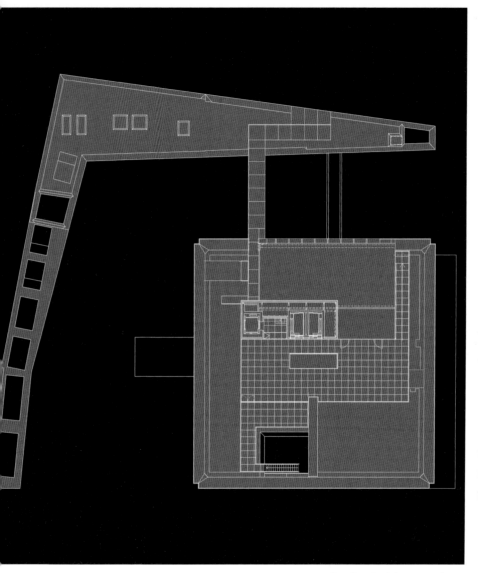

Level 11 Roof (+26.60 m)

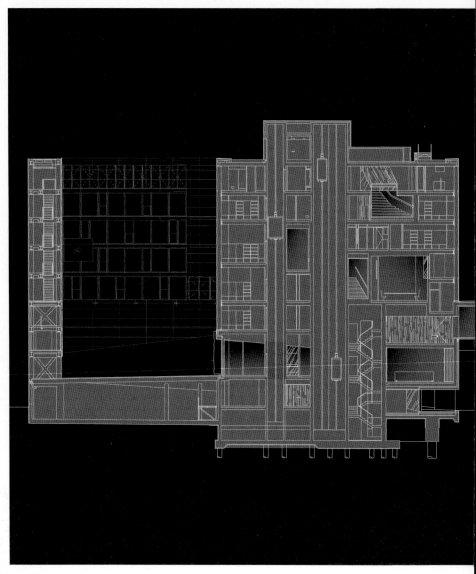

A East-We

Levels and Sections

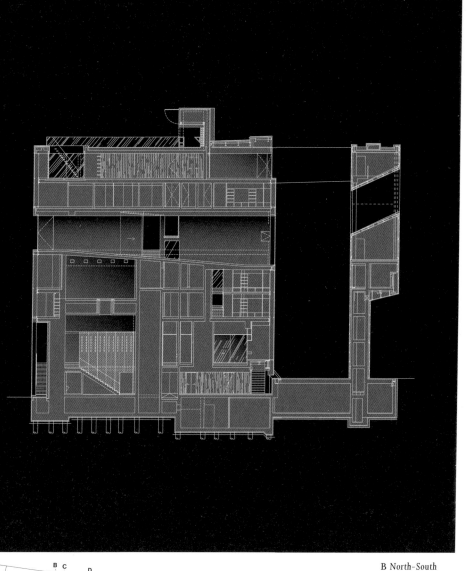

B North-South

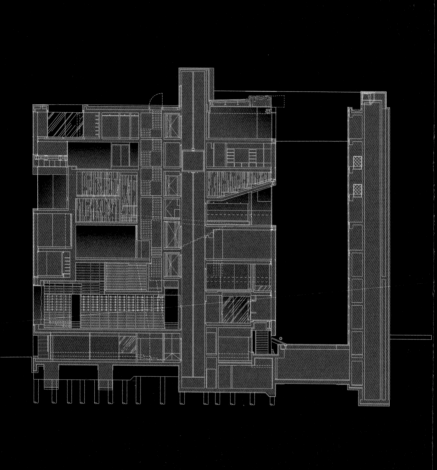

C North-Sou

Levels and Sections

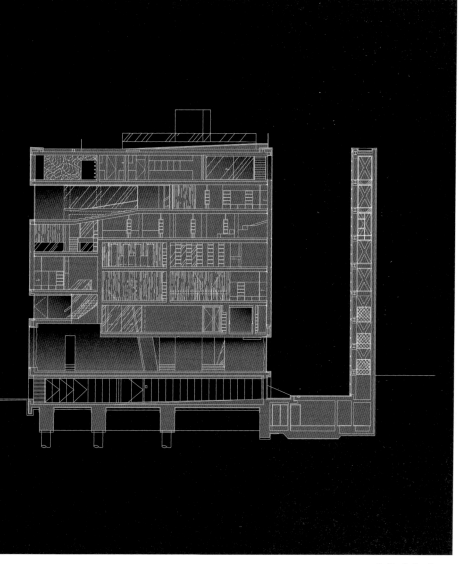

D North-South

Plates [2]

Candida Höfer

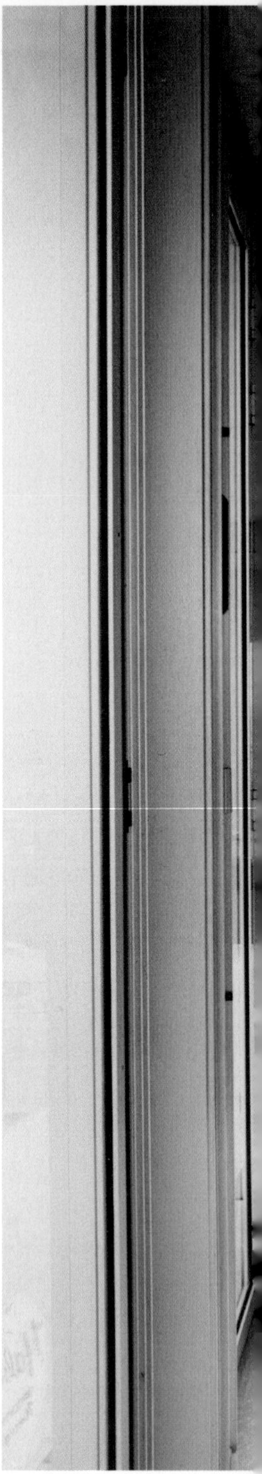

Building abroad

Dutch presence in Berlin: the Ministry of Foreign Affairs as client

Duc Boorsma and Ton van Zeeland

T.v.Z. (born in 1955) is an historian and cultural attaché with the Netherlands embassy in Berlin. He writes on historical and literary subjects and was one of the editors of the retrospective *Tweehonderd jaar Ministerie van Buitenlandse Zaken*, published in 1998.

D.B. (born in 1951) is an architect. He traded a corporate career for government service in 1990 and works at the Real Estate Abroad Department of the Ministry of Foreign Affairs as head of design and project management.

In the early 1990s, after the German federal government decided to move its seat from Bonn to Berlin, the idea of building a new Dutch Embassy in Berlin began to take shape. The result is a unique new Dutch building on the banks of the Spree.

But a lot happened before this result was achieved.

History

Before the Dutch Embassy in Bonn started to champion the country's interests in West Germany after the Second World War, the Netherlands was represented by a delegation seated in Berlin. This embassy was situated on Rauchstraße, in a building purchased in 1920. Before that, the Dutch delegation had been based at Number 16 Voßstraße in Berlin. The building on Voßstraße was, incidentally, torn down in the 1930s to make room for Hitler's Chancellery.

In 1920, entirely out of keeping with Dutch tradition, a number of buildings were purchased for the purposes of the Dutch international presence. A commission led by architect and Professor J.A.G. van der Steur was charged with the selection. Van der Steur was hardly an unknown – he had built, among other things, the Peace Palace in The Hague. Prof. van der Steur thought the property at Number 10 Rauchstraße appropriate; his only complaint was about the interior, which he considered tasteless.[1] The redecoration and renovation were undertaken by a Berlin architect. During the Second World War this building was obliterated by bombardments.[2] In 1973 the Netherlands sold the former embassy site on Rauchstraße to a private buyer.

After the embassy left Bonn in 1999, temporary accommodations were found in the Internationales Handels Zentrum (IHZ) building, a DDR-era high-rise in the centre of East Berlin. An embassy office had been located on its 23rd floor since 1995. The embassy was later housed on the 20th and 21st floors of this colossus.

More Presence

The Netherlands, as mentioned above, did not have a great or long-established tradition of erecting buildings abroad, or acquiring ownership of them. At the end of the twentieth century, however, thinking on this point had changed. The Netherlands wanted more recognition on the international scene, and this was expressed in many projects for building, renovating or decorating embassies. The choice of architect Rem Koolhaas and his team to design the new embassy in Berlin was partially influenced by this policy.

The Netherlands Goes Hunting in Berlin

By the time the ministry actually purchased the plot of land along the Spree, however, a lot of water had flowed under its bridges.

The beautifully situated site is located on Klosterstraße in the Mitte borough of Berlin. The Netherlands was originally offered sites and buildings far from the city centre. In 1994, however, a letter from Ambassador van Walsum to the Secretary-General of the Ministry of Foreign Affairs in The Hague made it clear that in fact the Netherlands' new embassy could only be situated in Tiergarten or Mitte.

The empty lot in Mitte was 'found' by the staff of the Berlin embassy office at the time. The embassy itself was still located in Bonn, as was the German government, and a sort of advance post, known as the embassy office, had been set up in Berlin in the IHZ building.

There was genuine pride in having tracked down such a fine plot of land. A multitude of contacts had been established at every level. For it was still unclear how things stood as far as ownership was concerned: could there be a claim dating from the Second World War? Nor was a claim to the property originating in the former DDR an impossibility. All of this was looked into and it became increasingly clear that the site was 'available' in more ways than one.

The Netherlands Builds in Berlin

The Berlin embassy office found a willing ear in The Hague, at the Real Estate Abroad Department, which is in charge of establishing and maintaining Embassy Buildings and Residences. In accordance with various architecture policy reports issued by the Dutch government, the Real Estate Abroad Department had drawn up a precise policy statement. This document is aimed at providing the Netherlands with recognizable buildings that reflect the nation's cultural achievements in the area of architecture and interior design.[3]

Not a simple brief, to be sure. The document spells out in quite some detail and in a rational way the requirements a Dutch diplomatic building should satisfy, thereby laying the foundations for architec-

128

ture of high quality for the ministry's buildings abroad. Important elements are formulated in terms of use value and cultural value without losing sight of exploitation costs. The document clearly indicates that the State and therefore certainly the Ministry of Foreign Affairs has a significant exemplary function. High quality requirements are formulated for the architecture as well as the decoration and design of the inside of the building. This is expressed, among other things, in the required high quality of the materials used and, for instance, the technical installations, which must meet high standards in connection with the energy conservation deemed necessary.

First Steps and Definitive Selection

A Europe-wide call for entries by architects and architecture firms was issued. The Government Architect, Wytze Patijn, was involved in the final selection. The premise was that the project should, insofar as is possible, be executed by a single consultancy firm or association. This form of consultancy is known as 'total engineering'. It was deemed important that the contestants display a broad and interesting vision and that they present a plan of approach, all in accordance with the programme of requirements. The setting of the building was to be considered part of the brief.

The selection took place in 1996. A programme of requirements was developed in accordance to the previously mentioned policy statement on real estate abroad and the specific demands of the department in The Hague for a delegation in Germany, a neighbouring country considered to be of particular significance.

Embassy in Berlin Represents the Netherlands

Given the great economic interests of the Netherlands in Germany, the departmental leadership in The Hague felt it vital that the Netherlands distinguish itself. The new location should not only be functional, but also representational. Besides a beautiful building site, the appearance and special facilities are also of great importance. These aspects are necessary as 'tools' for the embassy staff in fulfilling promoting the Netherlands activities, on the one hand and their other, more diplomatic duties on the other. The appearance of the building should reflect the hospitality and openness of the Netherlands, as well as its cultural standards.

These specific ideas can be read as a declaration of principles: aggressively geared toward presence and quality. A quote from the programme of requirements:

The obligation to 'just act normal' is the greatest scourge of Dutch culture; Dutch complacency has resulted in modernism turning into a style purely of reflex. At this very moment, on this spot, the in-depth exploration and reconsideration of a number of technical questions could have a regenerative effect, and create a distinct profile for the Netherlands in relation to the rest of Europe as well – less rhetoric and more action.

Through a preset rating point system in which other professional disciplines besides architecture were involved, the eventual winner of the selection was the OMA (Office for Metropolitan Architecture) association of architects led by Rem Koolhaas.

Now the declaration of principles described above could be turned into reality by OMA's designs.

Koolhaas's Vision

The selection committee was impressed by Koolhaas's and his team's vision. They did not want to build a ten-a-penny building, but rather to rebel against the regular and the all too normal. This was well received and understood at the ministry in The Hague at the time and it fit in brilliantly with the policy intentions set down in the real estate policy statement. An interesting point in this regard is that Koolhaas had previously distanced himself from a project in the City of Berlin because he felt the ideas on architecture expressed in that project would not lead to a new surge in modernism.

In the programme of requirements for the new Dutch Embassy in Berlin, Koolhaas grabbed the opportunity of a new chance and proclaimed: 'A new architecture that aims to be an advocate of the extraordinary within the everyday, a call to become so ambitious that one wants to bring the city and architecture into equilibrium with each other on a higher plane.' Koolhaas's design was presented in public at the Aedes architecture gallery, a big event that attracted a large audience.

130

A number of exceptional projects have been engendered by the policy direction and the implementation of Dutch construction policy. There is one very clear example: the Dutch Embassy in Berlin, by Rem Koolhaas and OMA. In fact the Ministry of Foreign Affairs has made it possible for Koolhaas to demonstrate in Berlin what he is trying to accomplish with his ideas on architecture after all.

Problems are Resolved Through Consultations
Cultural differences as well as the complexity and compatibility of a very unusual Dutch design in a Berlin setting are a few of the causes that can be identified for the delays in the construction process. In a process analogous to the Dutch polder model, however, the construction reached a successful conclusion under the motto *'Zusammenarbeit ist die neue Botschaft'* ('Cooperation is the new message'). One of Koolhaas's key phrases in the programme of requirements: 'the in-depth exploration and reconsideration of a number of technical questions' has certainly acquired a meaning of its own in that sense.

The Netherlands is Proud of the New Building
The completion of the Dutch Embassy in Berlin marks the culmination of a unique project that has already set many tongues wagging. The building fully meets all the representative ambitions specified and illustrates not only the Netherlands' vision on an urban design and architectural challenge, but our qualities in the domain of interior architecture, industrial design and art. Through it, the Netherlands not only shows it is capable of conceiving and outlining beautiful and daring plans, but also demonstrates the Dutch quality of successfully seeing things through.

1   Recently my esteemed colleague Bert van der Zwan, keeper of the historical function of the department, found a unique dossier. Thanks to him and this dossier a little corner of the history of pre-war buildings belonging to the Netherlands in Berlin can be illuminated. My thanks to Bert van der Zwan. In due time a more extensive account of the Dutch buildings in Berlin will be available.

2   Vincent Kramers, 'Het gezantschap te Berlijn in 1939 en 1940' in Erwin te Bokkel, Harm Hazewinkel and Ton van Zeeland (eds.), BZ en de Tweede Wereldoorlog, Den Haag 1995, pp. 7-10.

3   'Vastgoed in beweging, het huisvestingsbeleidsplan 1997 – 2001', The Hague, sa.

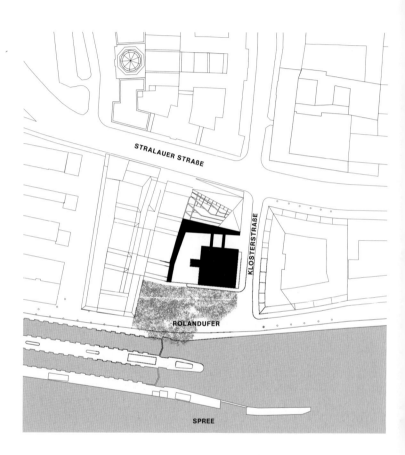

4-5 North façade with the view tunnel seen from the Stralauer Straße

6-7 South façade from the Spree

8-9 Exterior ramp, sky bridges connecting the residence to the Embassy building

10-11 Trajectory space above the residence entrance

12-13 View tunnel of the residence looking at the Alexander television tower

14-15 Atrium space framed by the residence and the Embassy building

16-17 East façade of the residence facing the Embassy across the atrium space

18-19 The main entrance of the west façade of the Embassy

20-21 West façade

22-23 The skybox over the atrium space

24-25 South façade

68-69 Foyer – the trajectory starting point

70-71 Trajectory to the cultural department

72-73 Trajectory ramp projecting out over the Klosterstraße

134

74-75 Trajectory re-entering the building

76-77 Trajectory proceeding through the view tunnel towards the Alexander television tower

78-79 Trajectory on the VIP level

80-81 Trajectory meeting the façade, looking towards the Spree

82-83 Trajectory passing by the fitness room

84-85 Trajectory towards the dining hall

86-87 East wall of the multipurpose room

88-89 Multipurpose room with view of the Spree

90-91 Archives

92-93 Office space under the trajectory

94-95 Offices

96-97 Partition wall of the offices

98-99 Perforated aluminium skin of the partition wall

100-101 WC entrance

102-103 Office

104-105 Large meeting room

106-107 Skybox from the Ambassador's level

108-109 Skybox

110-111 Mirror cube of the fitness room

112-113 Industrial kitchen, connected to the apartment of the deputy chef de mission

114-115 Break room over the trajectory

116-117 Travertine wall of the apartment of the deputy chef de mission

118-119 View from the Klosterstraße

120-121 View of the multipurpose room

122-123 Night view of the trajectory

124-125 Night view

The building

Project
  The Royal Netherlands Embassy
Status
  Commission 1997
  Completion 2003
Client
  Netherlands Ministry of Foreign
  Affairs – Real Estate Abroad Depart-
  ment, The Hague
Location
  Berlin-Mitte, Rolandufer / Kloster-
  straße
Site
  Facing street corner, park and river-
  front
Program
  8,500m²: offices 4,800m²; housing
  1,500m²; parking 2,200m²

Principal
  Rem Koolhaas
Project Directors
  Ellen van Loon, Erik Schotte
Project Architect
  Michelle Howard, Gro Bonesmo
Team
  Beth Margulis, Anu Leinonen, Daan
  Oievaar, Robert Choeff, Christian
  Muller, Adrianne Fisher, Oliver
  Schutte, Fernando Romero Havaux,
  Matthias Hollwich, Katrin Thorn-
  hauer, Barbara Wolff, Bruce Fisher,
  Anne Filson, Udo Garritzman, Jenny
  Jones, Mette Bos, Adam Kuhrdahl, Stan
  Aarts, Julien Desmedt, Annick Hess,
  Rombout Loman, Antti Lassila,
  Thomas Kolbasenko, Moritz von Voss,
  Paolo Costa, Carolus Traenkner,
  Susanne Manthey, Christiane Sauer,
  Tammo Prinz, Nils Lindhorst, Felix
  Thoma, Shadi Rahbaran
Research
  Bill Price, Marc Guinand

Structure
  Royal Haskoning / Arup Berlin
Services
  Huygen Elwako / Arup Berlin
Project Management
  Royal Haskoning
Fire
  Hosser Hass + Partner, Berlin
Lighting
  OVI, Washington DC, Berlin
Curtains
  Inside-Outside

The book

This publication was made possible thanks to the support of The Netherlands Ministry of Foreign Affairs – Real Estate Abroad Department, The Hague, The Dutch Embassy, Berlin

Concept
  Rem Koolhaas, Kayoko Ota (OMA),
  Véronique Patteeuw (NAi Publishers)
English copy-editing
  D'Laine Camp
English proofreading
  Pierre Bouvier
Translation
  Brian Holmes (Psychogeography of a Cube),
  Pierre Bouvier (Building abroad)
Photography
  Candida Höfer
Graphic design
  Coppens & Alberts
Printing and lithography
  Die Keure, Bruges
Production
  Brecht Bleeker (NAi Publishers)
Publisher
  Simon Franke (NAi Publishers)

Special thanks to Ralph Müller, Sabine Bürner and Shadi Rahbaran (OMA Berlin) for their help and cooperation; to Chantal Defesche, Rebecca Ehn and Mariëtte van Stralen (OMA) for their generosity and time.

Cover photo
  Candida Höfer

NAi Publishers is an internationally orientated publisher specialized in developing, producing and distributing books on architecture, visual arts and related disciplines.

www.naipublishers.nl
info@naipublishers.nl

It was not possible to find all the copyright holders of the illustrations used. Interested parties are requested to contact NAi Publishers, Mauritsweg 23, 3012 JR Rotterdam, The Netherlands.

Available in North, South and Central America through D.A.P./Distributed Art Publishers Inc, 155 Sixth Avenue 2nd Floor, New York, NY 10013-1507, Tel 212 6271999, Fax 212 6279484.

Available in the United Kingdom and Ireland through Art Data, 12 Bell Industrial Estate, 50 Cunnington Street, London W4 5HB, Tel 208 7471061, Fax 208 7422319.

Printed and bound in Belgium
ISBN 90-5662-356-7

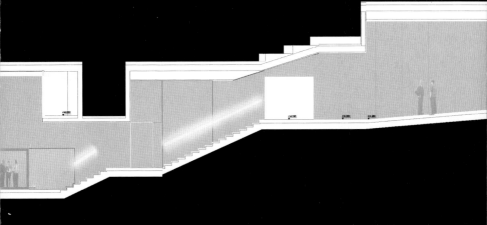

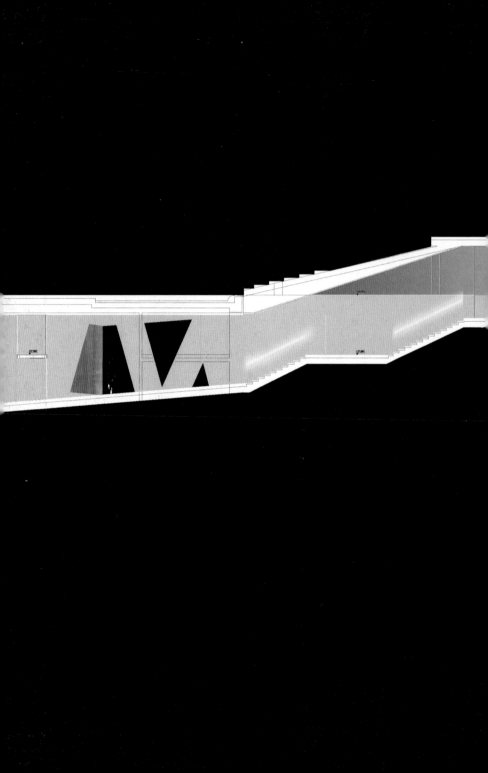